STEP-UP
SCIENCE

Keeping Warm

Louise and Richard Spilsbury

Evans

Published by Evans Brothers Limited
2A Portman Mansions
Chiltern Street
London W1U 6NR

© Evans Brothers Limited 2007

Produced for Evans Brothers Limited by
White-Thomson Publishing Ltd,
Bridgewater Business Centre,
210 High Street,
Lewes, East Sussex BN7 2NH

Printed in China by New Era Printing

Project manager: Rachel Minay

Designer: Flick, Book Design and Graphics

Consultant: Jackie Holderness,
Educational Consultant and Writer

The rights of Louise and Richard Spilsbury to be
identified as the authors of this work has been
asserted by the authors in accordance with the
Copyright, Designs and Patents Act 1988.

British Library Cataloguing in Publication Data

Keeping warm. - (Step-up science)
1. Cold adaptation - Juvenile literature 2. Body
temperature
591.4'2

ISBN-13: 9780237532093
ISBN-10: 0237532093

Acknowledgements:

The authors would like to thank Scott Fisher,
teacher at Stokenham Area Primary School for his
invaluable comments and advice on this series.

Picture acknowledgements:

pages 5bl (epa), 7l (FURGOLLE/Image Point
Royalty-Free), 14b (NASA/epa), 15b
(Vittoriano Rastelli), 16 main (Royalty-Free).
Ecoscene: pages 18b (Stephen Coyne), 19r (Chinch
Gryniewicz). iStockphoto.com: cover (tl), cover (tr),
title page, pages 4, 5br, 6t, 8b, 9t, 9b, 12, 13t,
15t, 16 inset, 18t, 20, 23t, 23t inset, 25l, 27t, 27b.
Martyn f. Chillmaid: pages 6b, 7r, 10–11, 11r, 17t,
17b, 23b. NHPA/Photoshot: cover (main), page
21b (Susanne Danegger). OSF/Photolibrary: page
21t (Daniel Cox). Science Photo Library: pages 13b
(Tony McConnell), 19l (Alfred Pasieka).

Illustrations by Ian Thompson (pages (5t, 14t, 22,
24, 25r, 26).

Contents

What is temperature?

Temperature is a measure of how hot or cold something is. When an object has a high temperature we say it is hot.

Touch and temperature

The skin provides us with our sense of touch. Nerve endings just beneath the surface of the skin send messages to the brain to tell us what things feel like. For example, when we touch different objects we notice whether they feel warm, very warm, cold or very cold. However, touch is not an accurate method of judging temperature, especially when there is only a small difference between temperatures. Also, some things are simply too hot or cold to touch safely.

Different temperatures

This thermometer shows the different temperatures of some familiar things. Draw a thermometer of your own with some of your own readings, such as the temperature of your bedroom, your own body temperature or your bathwater.

ice cubes

Hot or cold?

Prove that touch is not an accurate measure of temperature. Get three bowls of water, one very cold (add ice cubes), one lukewarm, and one very warm. Ask a friend to put one hand in the very warm water and one in the ice water (at the same time) for five seconds. Then ask them to put both hands in the lukewarm water. The water should feel warm to the hand that was in the cold water and cool to the hand that was in the hot water.

⚠️ SAFETY· Never touch ice immediately after it has been taken out of a freezer. For hot water, only use water that is very warm, so you don't burn yourself.

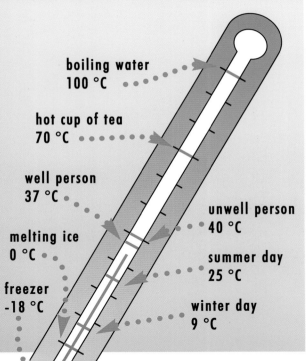

boiling water
100 °C

hot cup of tea
70 °C

well person
37 °C

unwell person
40 °C

melting ice
0 °C

summer day
25 °C

freezer
-18 °C

winter day
9 °C

What is a thermometer?

A thermometer is a device that measures the temperature of things exactly. There are different thermometers for measuring the temperature of different things, such as the air outside, the water in a swimming pool or the inside of a cooker. In homes and offices, there are temperature gauges (thermostats) attached to heating or air conditioning systems. The thermostats measure the temperature and control the heating or cooling systems, telling them when they need to make rooms cooler or warmer. A temperature sensor measures the temperature of the surrounding air.

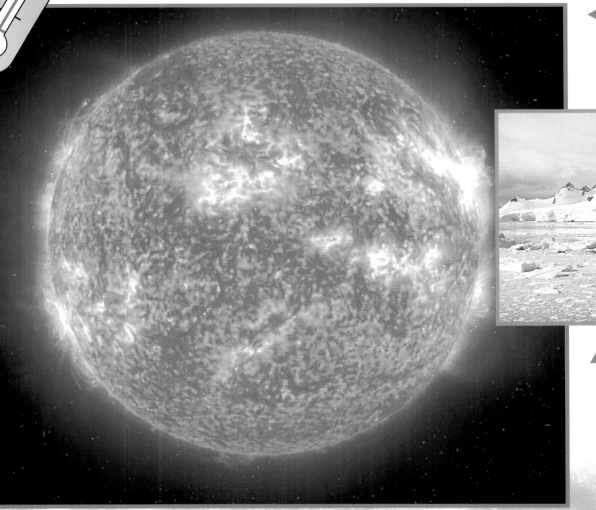

◀ The Sun, like all other stars in space, is a flaming ball of gases. It burns at 5,526 °C.

▲ Antarctica is the coldest place on Earth. The temperature here has dropped as low as -89 °C.

Measuring temperature

Although most thermometers use the same units, different thermometers work in different ways.

How does a bulb thermometer work?

Most room and outdoor thermometers have a long glass tube with a bulb at the bottom, filled with liquid. Liquids take up less space when cold and more space when warm. So if the temperature goes up, the liquid (usually a type of alcohol or a liquid metal called mercury) expands and moves up the tube.

liquid in bulb

How does a digital thermometer work?

A digital thermometer has an electronic temperature sensor inside that measures the temperature and shows the reading as a number on a digital display. Digital thermometers are often used to measure temperature inside the ear or under the tongue. These are good places to check body temperature because they are inside the body, so the thermometer reading is not affected by air temperature.

Why do we need to measure body temperature?

One of the most common uses of a thermometer is to check a person's body temperature. Normal body temperature is around 37 °C and any difference much above or below this is usually a sign of illness.

For example, hypothermia – when the body temperature drops below 35 °C – is very dangerous. A fever, which drives the body's temperature above 40 °C can also be very dangerous. If someone has a fever, steps need to be taken to cool them down, for example using fans or sponging the skin.

digital display

How does a forehead thermometer work?

A forehead thermometer is a heat-sensitive strip. A forehead thermometer has colour-changing numbers printed on its surface that react with the heat to show the temperature reading. Forehead thermometers are useful for measuring the temperature of a baby or someone who is asleep. In the thermometer below, blue indicates ½ °C above the temperature shown and red ½ °C below. What is the patient's temperature?

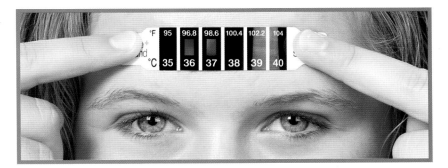

Make a thermometer

Use an old squeezy bottle and other bits and pieces to make your own thermometer and take some readings with it. You will find simple instructions at http://www.planet-science.com/experiment/text_expts/thermometer.html

SAFETY: Don't try to measure very hot or very cold things or you might hurt yourself.

▲ A digital thermometer like this one is inserted in the ear to give a quick and accurate reading of the patient's body temperature.

Heat energy

Heat is a form of energy. If heat is added to something, its temperature becomes higher. If heat is removed from something, its temperature becomes lower. If something is cold, it is because it has no heat energy.

Heat and temperature

Heat and temperature are not the same thing. Heat is energy and temperature is a measure of heat energy. The temperature of a warm cup of tea and a bath full of water might be the same, but the bathwater would have more heat energy because its volume would be greater. Or, looking at it another way, it takes a similar amount of heat energy to warm a whole bath of water to 25 °C as it does to boil a small kettle of water to 100 °C.

Each time a ball bounces, some of its movement energy is converted into heat energy. That is why the ball feels warmer when squash players finish a game of squash than it did before the game started.

Warm- and cold-blooded animals

Warm-blooded animals, including humans, generate their own heat from the inside so they stay at roughly the same temperature, even when their surroundings get cooler or warmer. Cold-blooded animals, such as lizards, snakes and tortoises, have to absorb the heat they need to be active from their surroundings. This is why you might see them lying out on a rock, warming up in the sunshine.

Friction, a force created when two things rub against each other, also causes heat. This is how we produce a flame when we strike a match against the rough side of a matchbox. Can you think of other examples of friction creating heat?

Sources of heat energy

There are many different sources of heat energy. Kinetic energy (also known as movement energy) creates heat, which is why people get warmer when they exercise. Heat energy from the Sun warms up the Earth. Plants use the Sun's energy to make and store their food. Fossil fuels such as coal, oil and gas are formed from plants that died millions of years ago. When they are burnt, for example to make electricity in power stations, energy is released that originally came from the Sun.

Changes of state

Heating a material can change its state, for example from a solid to a liquid, or a liquid to a gas. To boil water, we increase its temperature to 100 °C (boiling point). At this temperature, liquid water starts to change state and become steam. To make ice lollies, we decrease the temperature of flavoured water until it becomes very cold and reaches 0 °C (freezing point). At this temperature, liquid water changes state and becomes solid ice.

The day the Sun stopped shining ...

The Sun is the source of all Earth's warmth and light. Imagine what the world would be like without the Sun and write a story about 'The day the Sun stopped shining'.

How do things cool down?

Things cool down because of the way heat energy can transfer (move) from place to place. Heat always moves from an area where it is warmer to an area where it is colder. Heat spreads out from hotter things to cooler things until they are both the same temperature. Heat stops moving when the temperatures of two substances are even.

Room temperature

Because of the way heat moves, something hot will cool down and something cold will warm up until it is the same temperature as its surroundings. The average comfortable temperature of a room indoors is 20 °C. If a cup of hot chocolate and a glass of iced water are left in a room, both drinks will end up at the same temperature. Heat is lost from the surface of the hot drink until it reaches room temperature. Warmth from the room melts the ice and warms up the cold drink until it reaches room temperature as well.

▲ Heat flows out of a hot drink and into a cold drink until the two drinks are both the same temperature as their surroundings.

Recording temperatures

Predict the temperature of a jar of hot water and a jar of cold water after an hour in the same room. How often will you measure the temperature of the two jars of water? Record your results in a line graph. How can you explain the results?

Heat flow and the human body

Sometimes people have to cool down to keep the steady body temperature needed to be healthy. When we feel hot, the blood vessels just beneath the surface of the skin dilate, or get bigger. This increases the blood flowing near the surface and is the reason why we may look red in the face. Heat from the blood escapes, or flows out, from the skin into the air, helping us to feel cooler.

▲ *The next time someone complains you are letting cold air in, you can explain that actually warm air flowing out is making them feel colder.*

Line graphs are very useful for showing information that changes continuously over time. This line graph shows the changes in temperature in a place over 12 hours. What does it tell you about how the temperature changes throughout the day?

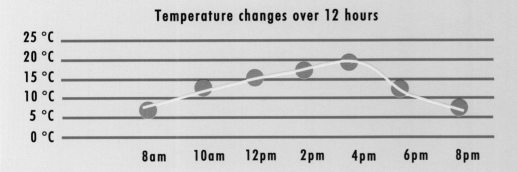

Temperature changes over 12 hours

Heat conduction

The way heat flows between materials that are touching is called conduction. Touching something hot can burn you because heat is conducted, or flows, from that object into your hand. When meat, fish or vegetables are fried in a pan, heat from the gas or electric hob flows through the pan by conduction to cook the food.

▼ *Saucepans have to be made from good heat conductors, such as steel, iron or copper, so they heat food evenly and quickly.*

Good thermal conductors

Materials that let heat pass through them are called thermal conductors. Good thermal conductors let heat pass through them easily. They heat up and cool down very quickly. Metals, such as iron and copper, are good thermal conductors. When you touch a metal doorknob or railing, heat from your hand flows easily into the metal. Because your hand is losing heat, the metal feels cold to the touch.

How does conduction explain why you can burn your hand on a metal spoon left in a pan of boiling water or hot, bubbling sauce? Why don't wooden spoons get hot when they are left in a hot pan?

Poor thermal conductors

Some substances conduct heat more easily than other substances. Poor thermal conductors, also called thermal insulators, are substances that warm up and cool down very slowly. Poor thermal conductors include rocks and stone, fabrics and plastics.

▲ *Metal slides usually feel cold because the metal conducts heat away from the skin. But on hot summer days, the metal absorbs the Sun's heat quickly and slides can feel very hot to the touch.*

So, for example, hot chocoloate or soup from a takeaway stand is often served in a polystyrene cup. Polystyrene is a kind of plastic so it protects your hands from the hot liquid. And although saucepans are often made of metal, because metal conducts heat to the food inside quickly, saucepan handles are usually made from wood or plastic because these materials stop heat flowing into your hand.

Conduction experiment

Plan an investigation to find out which materials conduct heat best. Put three spoons – one metal, one wood, and one plastic – into a jug of hot tap water. What do you think will happen? Touch them after one minute and again after two minutes. Were you correct? Try this activity again, first putting a small piece of cold butter on top of each spoon. Which spoon melts the butter first? What does this prove?

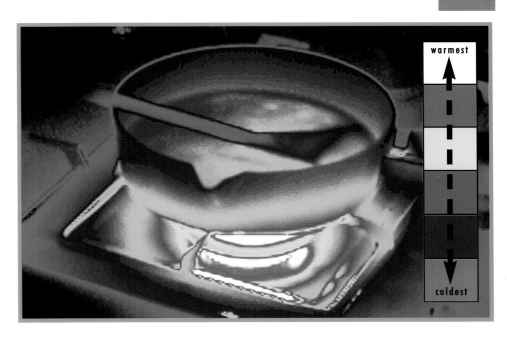

▲ *This is a thermogram, an image that shows variations in temperature. Use the colour key to see which parts are hotter and which colder. For example, the pan (probably made of metal) is a good conductor and the spoon (probably plastic or wood) is a poor conductor.*

Heat insulation

A conductor allows heat to pass through it but an insulator does not. Insulators stop the flow of heat from warm areas to cold areas. Thermal insulators cannot make a cold thing warm, they can only hold in warmth that is already there. A cold stone wrapped up in a fluffy blanket or duvet will stay cold, but a warm-blooded human, wrapped in a duvet, will stay warm. The duvet acts as an insulator and stops the heat flowing out of the person's body.

Insulating materials

Some substances are better at insulating than others. Materials that are poor conductors of heat, such as wood, plastic and paper, make good insulators. Another good insulator is air. Trapped air insulates very effectively. For example, oven gloves protect hands from a hot oven because the layers of thick fabric in the gloves have fibres that trap air in them. A thermos flask keeps soup warm because it has two sections that trap a layer of insulating air.

Can you explain why bubble wrap is a better insulator than cling film?

A concept map shows the links between ideas around a particular topic. Where would you put 'sleeping bag' on this concept map?

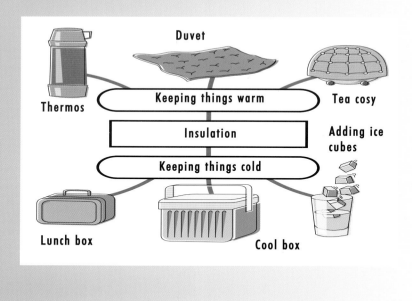

Thermos — Duvet — Tea cosy

Keeping things warm

Insulation — Adding ice cubes

Keeping things cold

Lunch box — Cool box

▼ *These thermal protection tiles are just one of seven different layers of insulation material on a space shuttle, needed to protect the inside from the intense 1,649 °C heat caused by friction between the spacecraft and the Earth's atmosphere as astronauts return to Earth.*

Keeping food cold keeps it fresh for longer. If you don't have an insulated lunch box or coolbag, try using two paper bags to insulate your cold snacks.

Insulating cold things

Insulators not only keep warm things warm, but they can also keep cool things cool. Because heat cannot pass easily through layers of insulation, a well-insulated cold substance will remain cold. A polystyrene lunch box will keep drinks or a packed lunch cool because polystyrene is a good thermal insulator. Wrapping a tub of ice cream in newspaper helps to stop it from melting too soon. Layers of air, trapped between the sheets of newspaper, insulate the ice cream and help to keep it cold.

Test the insulation

How do different materials affect the melting time of an ice cube? Take five identical ice cubes. Leave one unwrapped, then wrap each of the others in a single layer of one of the following: newspaper, greaseproof paper, aluminium foil and bubble wrap. Secure them with an elastic band. Put them in the same place and see how quickly they melt. Why do you need to leave one ice cube unwrapped? Record your results in a table. Which material made the best insulator? Why?

Insulated containers are vital when transporting organs for transplant. In this picture, a kidney has arrived by plane for a transplant operation.

Electrical conductors and insulators

Like heat, electricity is a kind of energy and when electricity flows, it makes things heat up. Just as heat is conducted more easily through some materials than through others, so is electricity. The materials that make good thermal conductors and insulators also often make good electrical conductors and insulators.

What conducts electricity?

Just as a thermal conductor is a material that lets heat travel through it easily, a material that electricity travels through is called an electrical conductor. Most metals are both good thermal conductors and electrical conductors. Metal cables and wires carry mains electricity from a power station, where electricity is made, all the way to the sockets in our walls. And the prongs ••••➤ on plugs are made of metal to conduct electricity from sockets into electrical appliances such as computers and kettles.

▶ *An iron has a heating element inside that converts electrical energy to heat energy. The heat is controlled by a thermostat which switches the electric current on and off to keep the iron at the selected temperature.*

Insulators for protection

Materials that electricity cannot travel through easily are called electrical insulators. Rubber, plastic, glass, ceramics and wood are all good electrical insulators since electric currents do not travel through them easily. Electrical insulators are used for protection. Most electric cables, plugs and sockets have plastic coatings to stop the electricity moving through the metal and into people.

How does this explain why metal tools, such as drills, have handles made of plastic, rubber or wood?

▼ Which parts of the appliances in this picture are metal and which are plastic? In each case can you say why those particular materials were chosen?

Testing circuits

Set up your own experiment to test materials for conductivity. Go to http://www.digitalbrain.com /document.server/ subjects/ks2sci/su4 /mod1/circuit.htm for instructions.

This site also has more information about electric circuits and other activity ideas.

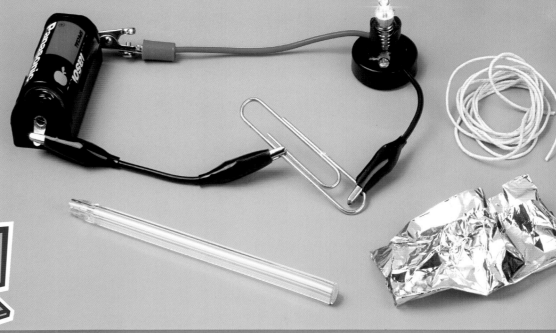

▲ Which of the materials in this picture could be used to complete the circuit and conduct the electricity to light the bulb and which could not?

How do we keep warm?

We know that it is important for people to maintain an even body temperature so they stay healthy. But how can we do this when seasons change and winter often brings very cold weather?

Clothes for warmth

People stop themselves losing warmth by wearing insulating clothes. Wool feels warm because it traps the warm air escaping from the body in its fibres. Wearing lots of thin layers can keep a person warmer than one thick layer because air is trapped between the layers. Approximately half a person's body heat is lost through the head, which is why it helps to wear a hat in winter.

Absorbing and reflecting heat

On a sunny day, have you ever noticed that you feel warmer in a black T-shirt than a white one? Dark and dull colours absorb, or soak up, more heat than light-coloured objects so they feel hotter. Many people in hot countries paint their houses white because light colours, and shiny surfaces, reflect heat rays away.

How could you test this using two thermometers and two boxes, one covered in black paper and one covered with white paper?

▲ Snowboarders and skiers often wear feather-filled clothes to keep the heat in.

And keeping cool ...

It is just as important to find ways of keeping cool in hot weather as it is to keep warm in cold weather. In many hot places people wear layers of white cotton clothing to keep cool. The white colour reflects heat and the loose clothes trap a layer of air that stops warmth being conducted to their bodies.

Keeping homes warm

It costs money to heat our homes. We can spend less if we stop the heat from radiators and heaters escaping. A layer of insulation (fibreglass padding or special foam) between brick walls helps to hold in heat and many windows have double-glazing. In double-glazed windows, the two layers of glass trap a layer of air between them to stop heat flowing out of them so easily.

▼ *This thermogram shows heat loss from a house. The yellow of the roof and windows shows they are losing the most heat, while the walls are losing the least.*

In this picture, recycled newspaper is being sprayed into the gap between walls to insulate the building.

Energy detectives

Be an energy detective! Find out how your home is already insulated to keep it warm. Then think of at least three ways to improve the insulation of your home and save energy.

How do animals keep warm?

People can change their clothes to keep warm or turn up the heating in their well-insulated homes, but how do animals that live in extremely cold places keep warm?

Insulating layers

Mammals (animals that give birth to live young) and birds are warm-blooded. This means that they try to maintain a constant body temperature, even when they are in a cold environment. Some mammals that live in the cold depths of the sea, such as seals and whales, have a thick layer of blubber (fat) under the skin to keep them warm.

Wear a blubber glove

Make a blubber glove at http://www.planetscience.com. This site tells you how to fill rubber gloves with vegetable fat. If you put your hand in a bowl of very cold water while wearing the blubber glove you'll be able to see how efficiently a layer of fat can insulate a body.

◀ Whales are warm-blooded mammals that live permanently in cold water. They manage to keep warm, even in the icy seas around Antarctica, because of the thick insulating layer of fat just below their skin. One of the reasons whales have to find and eat such large amounts of food is to maintain this heavy blubber.

Mammals have hair or fur. Birds have feathers. When animals move their muscles, they make heat that warms air above the skin. This warm air is trapped by fur or feathers to form a layer of insulation. In very cold weather, birds also fluff up their feathers to trap more air. In colder places mammals have longer hair. Many grow extra hair in the winter and then moult (shed hair) when temperatures warm up in spring.

Nests and burrows

Some animals make burrows under the ground to avoid cold. Although ice and snow are very cold, they make good insulators because they trap a lot of air. In the Arctic, voles live in a network of tunnels under the snow, eating underground roots along the way and polar bears dig dens in the snow to give birth to their cubs or to escape the coldest spells of weather. Some animals hibernate to avoid the coldest winter months. They find a safe, warm place and curl up for a long sleep-like rest. Hedgehogs and many other animals line their nests with layers of twigs, moss and leaves to create their own insulation.

▲ *The arctic fox has a winter coat of dense white fur, which helps it to survive freezing temperatures. It sheds its thick fur for a grey-brown coat in summer.*

▶ *During hibernation, an animal's heartbeat and body functions slow down. An animal such as this dormouse would not be able to keep warm enough to survive cold winters outside its insulated nest.*

Heat and Planet Earth

Planet Earth is a ball of rock and metal in space. The outer layer is called the crust and is divided up in to seven gigantic plates, or slabs, of cool solid rock. Although we cannot feel these plates moving, they are shifting slightly all the time, as they float on the liquid rock, melted by the intense heat in the core, or centre of the Earth.

Making mountains

Hot liquid rock from the core of the Earth rises, then cools and spreads out nearer the surface and sinks to be heated again. This movement is called convection and it causes the plates on top to move as well. Most mountains, including the Alps and the Himalayas, which formed about 50 million years ago, were created when the movements of the liquid rock caused two plates to collide with each other. Over millions of years, this caused land at the edges of both plates to fold up and form high peaks, which we call mountains.

Crust

Mantle

Inner core

Outer core

▲ This cross-section shows Earth's layers. The mantle is a layer of slowly flowing molten (melted) rock. The outer core is mostly liquid metal and the inner core is a mix of solid and liquid metal.

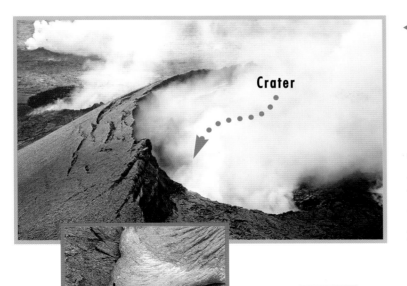

Crater

Lava

When a volcano erupts, hot lava bursts out of the crater. Lava cools and hardens forming the sides of a volcano, called the cone.

Geothermal energy

The Earth's natural heat is called geothermal energy. In geothermal power plants cold water is pumped deep underground, where it is heated by dry hot rocks and is pumped back to the surface. The steam is used in power stations to make electricity.

Research solar energy

Geothermal energy is a cleaner energy source than coal or oil because it doesn't make air pollution. It is also a form of renewable energy, which means it won't run out. Research solar power, another form of clean, renewable heat energy.

Volcanoes

Volcanoes form when some of the magma, or hot liquid rock, underground squeezes up through gaps between the Earth's plates. It gets stuck below the crust and as more and more liquid rock rises, the pressure builds up. Then, suddenly, the volcano erupts and hot rock bursts through the crust. In the air, the liquid rock cools and sets into hard rock, often forming a mountain.

The water in this lagoon in Iceland is from the geothermal power plant that can be seen in the background. The plant pumps up hot water from the Earth and uses it to make electricity. Any clean water that is left over flows into the lagoon.

Temperatures around the world

Heat energy moves by conduction when objects touch. Heat and light from the Sun travels to Earth in invisible straight lines. This is called radiation. But if the Sun heats the whole planet, why do temperatures differ around the world?

Hot and cold

The Sun's rays travel to Earth in straight lines, but the Earth is a sphere (ball shape) so its surface is curved. This means the rays hit the ground at different angles. They hit the area round the Equator, the imaginary line around the centre of the Earth, straight on, making this the hottest part of the Earth. But they hit the Poles at a slanting angle. The warmth is spread out over a wider area, making these the coolest places on Earth.

High and low

The altitude, or height above or below sea level, also affects the average temperature of a place. The Sun's heat warms up the land and the oceans. The warm land and sea heat the air above them, and this air warms air higher up and so on. Higher in the atmosphere there is less heat available so it is colder.

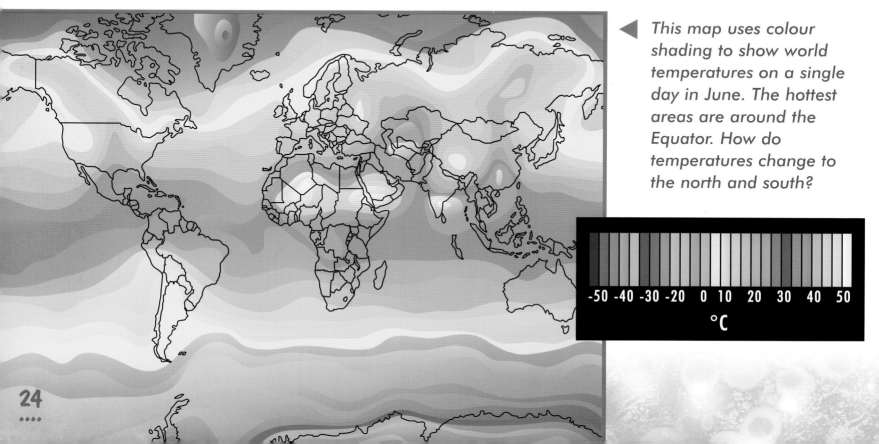

◄ This map uses colour shading to show world temperatures on a single day in June. The hottest areas are around the Equator. How do temperatures change to the north and south?

-50 -40 -30 -20 0 10 20 30 40 50
°C

The temperature drops about 3 °C every 500 metres up a mountain, which is why mountain peaks are very cold and always covered in snow.

▲ *Even in hot countries of the world it is cold at the top of a mountain because air gets colder as you get higher in the air. Climbers take thick sleeping bags and windproof tents to keep them warm.*

Night and day

Why is it cooler at night than during the day? Earth makes one complete rotation, or turn, on its axis every 24 hours. During this rotation, half of the Earth is facing the Sun and has daytime. The other half faces away from the Sun, so it has night. It feels warmer in the day than at night because in the day we feel warmth

Night and day

This diagram shows how the rotation of the Earth on its axis gives us day and night. You can also see how the Sun's rays hit the area around the Equator or centre of the Earth directly, making this area hot. The Poles are colder because the Sun's rays hit them at an angle and spread out over a wider area.

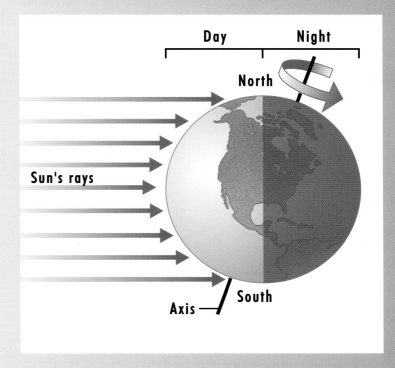

from the Sun. The only warmth we feel at night comes from heat absorbed by the land during the day. The rotation of Earth seems to make the Sun move across the sky during daytime but the Sun really isn't moving at all. The Earth rotates around its own axis as it orbits the Sun.

Changing temperatures

Many scientists believe that the world's climate is changing. They predict that temperatures will get hotter all around the world. They call this global warming.

Greenhouse effect

The atmosphere is a blanket of mixed gases that surrounds Earth. Some of these gases are known as greenhouse gases. They keep our planet at a temperature that allows us to live.

When heat from the Sun hits the Earth's surface, much of it then reflects away into the sky. Greenhouse gases stop some of the Sun's warmth escaping back into space and reflect the heat back towards Earth.

The greenhouse effect keeps the average surface temperature of the Earth at about 15 °C. Without greenhouse gases the Earth would be as cold as the surface of the Moon, which is about -18 °C.

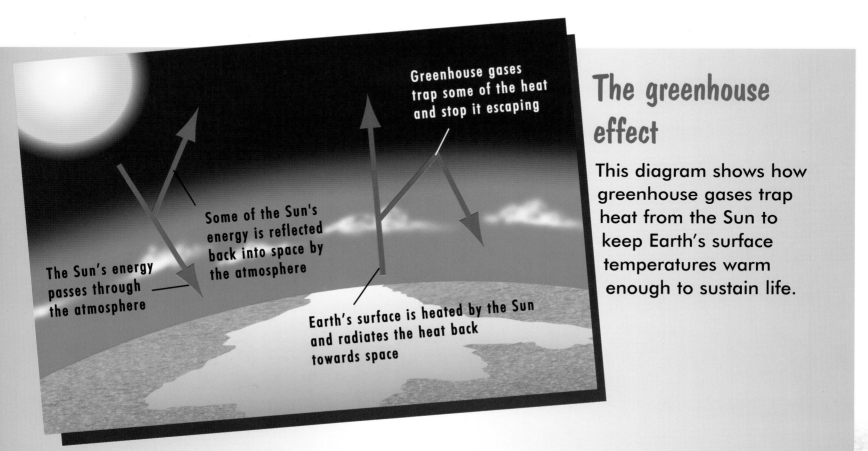

Greenhouse gases trap some of the heat and stop it escaping

Some of the Sun's energy is reflected back into space by the atmosphere

The Sun's energy passes through the atmosphere

Earth's surface is heated by the Sun and radiates the heat back towards space

The greenhouse effect

This diagram shows how greenhouse gases trap heat from the Sun to keep Earth's surface temperatures warm enough to sustain life.

Global warming

When we burn fossil fuels (coal, oil and gas) we dramatically increase the amount of greenhouse gases, such as carbon dioxide, in the atmosphere. The extra greenhouse gases trap too much heat and scientists believe that, on average, world temperatures may increase by 6 °C by the end of the 21st century. This may not sound like a big increase, but it would affect rainfall, melt ice caps and increase sea levels. It may also increase the number and strength of extreme weather events such as storms and floods. These effects would have a serious impact on plants, wildlife and people.

▲ *One result of global warming may be that polar bears become extinct, or die out. Polar bears hunt seals from floating platforms of ice in the sea. As these melt, some bears starve; others drown if they have to swim too far to find food.*

▲ *Many people are already using alternative sources of energy, such as wind and solar power. This wind farm produces electricity without burning fossil fuels.*

In the future

There are many ways individuals and countries can reduce the effects of global warming. Governments can find ways to reduce the amount of electricity people use, for example by encouraging people to insulate their homes. People are more aware of the carbon dioxide produced by cars and using alternative forms of transport. What are you, your family or your school doing to make a difference?

Glossary

absorb   to soak up.

altitude   the height above sea level.

atmosphere   the blanket of air (gases, including oxygen) that surround Planet Earth.

axis   an imaginary line about which the Earth rotates.

circuit   a closed loop or circle, usually of wire, through which electricity flows.

climate   usual patterns of weather in an area year after year.

conduction   the transfer of energy through a substance or from one substance to another when they touch.

convection   the way heat is carried by a gas or liquid.

crust   the hard, cool outer layer of Planet Earth.

electricity   a form of energy that we use to power a variety of machines, from computers to ovens.

energy   the ability to do work. Heat energy is a type of energy that flows when there are differences in temperature.

Equator   an imaginary line around the centre of the Earth.

fossil fuels   fuels that formed from the remains of plants and animals that died millions of years ago.

friction   a force that resists motion between two objects that rub against each other.

geothermal energy   heat generated by natural processes within the Earth.

global warming   the general increase in world temperatures.

greenhouse effect   describes the way the Sun's heat energy is trapped in Earth's atmosphere.

hibernate   to go into a deep sleep to survive cold winters.

ice cap   an area permanently covered in ice.

insulation   something that slows the transfer or flow of heat through a substance.

kinetic energy   movement energy.

mantle   the layer of the Earth between the crust and the core.

nerve endings   nerves carry messages to and from the brain in the human body. Nerve endings in the skin sense things like pain or heat and send messages about the feelings to the brain.

orbit   to travel in a circular or oval path around another object in space, for example the Moon orbits the Earth.

plates   rigid slabs that make up the Earth's crust.

thermometer a device that measures how hot or cold something is.

thermostat a thermometer that uses its temperature measurements to control equipment such as heating and cooling systems.

pollution contamination in the air, water or soil that harms human health or the environment.

radiation energy that travels in the form of rays or waves.

reflect to throw or bounce back.

renewable energy energy sources that are naturally and continually replenished so they will not run out.

room temperature a temperature of about 20 °C, at which people feel comfortable indoors.

temperature the measure of how warm or cold things are.

thermal conductor something that allows heat to pass through it easily.

thermal insulator something that doesn't allow heat to pass through it easily.

thermogram a picture that records variations in temperature.

For teachers and parents

This book is designed to support and extend the learning objectives for Unit 4C of the QCA Science Schemes of Work.

Throughout this book and throughout their own investigative work children should be aware that science is based on evidence and they should have the opportunity to:

- Turn questions into an investigation.
- Predict results.
- Understand the need to collect sufficient evidence.
- Understand the need to conduct a fair test.
- Choose and use appropriate measuring or investigation equipment.
- Record results using tables and bar charts, sometimes using ICT.
- Interpret evidence by making observations, comparisons and conclusions using scientific language.

There are opportunities for cross-curricular work in literacy, numeracy, design technology and ICT.

SAFETY

Do not use mercury thermometers because they are made of glass and there is a problem with cleaning up toxic mercury if they are broken.

When doing investigations, do not let children touch ice straight after it comes out of the freezer and only ever use hand-hot water, not very hot or boiling water.

SUGGESTED FURTHER ACTIVITIES

Pages 4 - 5 What is temperature?
Children could do the touch test for temperatures around school and make a list of which feel warm, very warm, cold or very cold.

Children could find out about Swedish astronomer Anders Celsius and German scientist Gabriel Fahrenheit, who gave their names to the temperature scales, by typing their names into a search engine or

looking at http://www.energyquest.ca.gov/how_it_works /thermometer.html

Useful information about temperature, thermometers and heat transfer can be found on the following website: http://eo.ucar.edu/skymath/tmp2.html

Pages 6 - 7 Measuring temperature
Children need lots of first-hand experience taking different temperatures using several different thermometers. They could also use temperature sensors to record the temperature of different spots around school over 24 hours and record results using ICT.

Children could draw a plan of the class (or school grounds), predict which part of the room is hottest and then label the plan with the actual measurements. Were they correct? Will the measurements change over time?

Pages 8 - 9 Heat energy
Warm and cold-blooded animals around the world: children could explore why there are many more reptiles and insects in hot Equatorial climates than in Arctic climates.

Pages 10 - 11 How do things cool down?
Children could play the 'Hotter or Colder?' game at http://www.bbc.co.uk/schools/podsmission/ solidsandliquids

Pages 12 - 13 Heat conduction
On a hot day, metal surfaces in playgrounds can heat up enough to burn the skin. Children could design a poster to warn younger children about this. As young children may not be able to read, they should think of a visual way of showing this. To help, they could brainstorm ideas about everyday symbols, such as those on lavatory doors, or 'No Smoking' signs.

Pages 14 - 15 Heat insulation
Children can also test the effect of different thermal insulators in keeping baked potatoes hot and make a graph with results. See: http://www.hitchams.suffolk.sch.uk/datalogging/ keeping_things_hot.htm

Children may find it difficult to accept that insulation keeps cold things cold as well as warm things warm. They could make a poster of ways we keep cold things cold and why we do so, for example to stop frozen foods from defrosting on the way home from the supermarket.

Pages 16 - 17 Electrical conductors and insulators

There is a very useful page of information about helping your KS2 child with the electricity topic at http://www.hep.phys.soton.ac.uk/hycs/electricity.pdf

Children could write a leaflet containing practical advice on keeping warm during a power cut. There are some suggestions at http://www.glps.net/pwrout/keepwarm.htm

Pages 18 - 19 How do we keep warm?

Children could write a computer program that turns a classroom heater on before they arrive in the morning and off for the night. This helps children to understand that devices can be controlled using a computer. They could use a control box simulation program to instruct a computer to turn the heater on and off at set times. They may need help writing the control language to produce the correct sequence.

Children could explore clothing materials further, using the computer to take temperature measures with sensors and a data logger. See: http://curriculum.becta.org.uk/docserver.php?docid=1456 and the related activity, 'Keeping cool' at http://curriculum.becta.org.uk/docserver.php?docid=1435

At http://kids.msfc.nasa.gov children can find out how an astronaut's spacesuit protects him or her from the extreme temperatures in outer space.

Pages 20 - 21 How do animals keep warm?

At http://www.planet-science.com/sciteach/start.html children can see how birds keep warm by fluffing up their feathers to create air pockets.

Children could also try the online quiz about keeping warm at http://www.planet-science.com/wired/index.html?page=/wired/comp_quiz/12_05/index.html

Pages 22 - 23 Heat and Planet Earth

At http://www.nhm.ac.uk/kids-only/fun-games/volcano/ children can find out how to build their own volcano and watch it erupt!

There is an interesting activity at http://www.dep.org.uk/activities/ge-activities/5/stayorleave/start.htm. Children pretend they live on Montserrat island under the threat of a volcano. They must explore reasons that people choose to stay in a crisis situation like this, or choose to leave.

Pages 24 - 25 Temperatures around the world

At http://www.bbc.co.uk/weather/world/ children can compare temperatures for places shown on maps across the world. The site also has features such as 'Ten Winter Sun Spots' in which children can compare places to find summer sunshine when it is winter at home.

The activity at http://curriculum.becta.org.uk/docserver.php?docid=1461 uses computer sensors to record light and temperature changes that happen in the classroom during night and day and has sample line graphs that can be made with results.

Pages 26 - 27 Changing temperatures

The ACE 'Global warming' activity pack has lots of information, activities and games for KS2 and 3 at http://www.ace.mmu.ac.uk/Resources/Teaching_Packs/Key_Stage_3/Global_Warming/pdf/Global_Warming.pdf

Index